CW01160850

THE DOG IN YOUR FAMILY

Marianne Mays

© 1999 Kingdom Books, PO Box 15, Waterlooville PO7 6BQ, England. All rights reserved. No part of this publication may be reproduced, stored in a retrieval system, or transmitted in any form or by any means, electronic, mechanical, photocopying, recording or otherwise, without the written permission of the publisher.

CONTENTS

Chapter 1 So your children want a dog? ... 4

Chapter 2 Choosing a dog 9

Chapter 3 Where to buy your dog 19

Chapter 4 Your new dog at home 27

Chapter 5 Your dog and a new baby 32

Chapter 6 Care and equipment 36

Chapter 7 Basic training 41

Index 48

SO YOUR CHILDREN WANT A DOG?

Chapter 1 So your children want a dog?

There cannot be many parents who never have had to listen to their children plead for a dog of their own. A cute little puppy, just like the one their best friend has got. A handsome Collie, just like the one they've seen on television. A clever Dalmatian, just like the ones on their favourite video. As a parent, it is all too easy to give in to children's pleas, either for the sake of a quiet life, or because you think it would be good for the children to grow up with a pet or because, secretly, you have always wanted a dog. However, taking on another family member, which a properly cared-for dog should become, is not something that ever should be undertaken lightly. If everything is to work out as well as all of you would like, it is not only important, but *essential*, that the subject is researched and discussed thoroughly before any decision is taken as to whether a dog should be acquired.

Company

The first question to be addressed is whether your particular circumstances make your family suitable as dog owners. Is somebody at home during the main part of the day? A dog, particularly a puppy, needs companionship and will not be happy left on his own for more than an absolute maximum of three or four hours a day. If all the family members are out at work or at school, then owning a dog is not a good idea. A lonely dog is a bored and unhappy dog that may take out its frustration on your home, chewing and soiling. Getting two dogs instead of one is not a solution as you simply end up with two bored dogs; dogs need human companionship. A young puppy that is undergoing the process of house-training cannot be left alone for more than a few minutes now and then. For the older puppy, training is needed to get him used to the idea of being left on his own for a few hours.

SO YOUR CHILDREN WANT A DOG?

Exercise

Where you live is another important question. Many rescue centres will rehome dogs only to people who live in a house with a secure garden, and some breeders may make a similar stipulation. It is very true to say that life as a dog owner will be much easier if you have your own garden, especially when house training a puppy, as it will be very easy to get the dog outside in no time at all to urinate and defecate. Letting the dog play in the garden must never be seen as a substitute for proper exercise, that is, regular walks. All adult dogs, regardless of breed, need at least one good walk every day whatever the weather. Many breeds will not be satisfied with less than an hour's good free running exercise. It is very cruel to acquire a dog and keep it more or less permanently in the back garden. Neither is it an option simply to let the dog out on the streets to exercise himself, as do owners of so-called 'latchkey' dogs. These dogs are a nuisance and a danger to themselves, other dogs and people, as they foul and, perhaps, cause accidents. Dogs need their daily walks; this must never be forgotten.

SO YOUR CHILDREN WANT A DOG?

It is fair to say that you can still own a dog even if you live in a flat. It is not the space inside your home or the size of garden that matters; it is how much exercise the dog is given. If you live in a flat without a garden, then you must be prepared to take your dog out for walks at least four times a day. Also make sure that pets are allowed where you live, as many flat landlords have a 'no pets' rule.

Some dogs may prefer to stay at home in front of the fire when it is raining, but most will love and demand their walk even if the weather is foul. Being a dog owner is not just for fair weather! It is a sad fact that many dog owners only seem to remember that they have a dog when the sun is shining. This is very unfair to the dog and you may end up with a bored, frustrated pet that will cause havoc in your home.

You will need to live within easy reach of some suitable exercise area, such as a park or common. It is no good living in the middle of a concrete jungle miles from the nearest park. Also check with your local council that dogs are allowed to be exercised in the parks as, sadly, more and more councils enforce dog bans.

SO YOUR CHILDREN WANT A DOG?

Does everyone want a dog?
Having made sure that somebody is at home during the day and that your living circumstances are suitable for owning a dog, the next question must be whether everyone in the family really wants to have one. **Never** be tempted to fall for the children's promises that they will look after and care for the dog of their dreams! Children lose interest quickly, and what may be their greatest interest one day can be completely forgotten the next. No child under the teenage years can, or should, be expected to take sole responsibility for a dog. The ultimate responsibility must always lie with you, the adult. Therefore, it is utterly pointless to acquire a dog unless everyone in the family is prepared to help out with all the practicalities. Even if it is agreed that Mum and the children will care for the dog, it is not right

SO YOUR CHILDREN WANT A DOG?

to get a pup if dad doesn't really like dogs and doesn't welcome the idea. A dog must be able to feel wanted and loved by all the family and, if one family member does not really like dogs, he or she is much more unlikely to feel able to tolerate the various problems that dog ownership invariably brings, such as muddy pawprints on the carpet, chewed objects or dog hairs on clothes. Talk about it as a family, discuss what owning a dog will entail and make a point of visiting friends with dogs or asking them round, to get a general idea of what life with a dog will be like. This will also ensure that no unpleasant surprises will be in store, such as someone finding out they are allergic to dog hair! It is always best to find out these things well before a dog comes into the home.

Cost of keeping a dog

Can you afford to keep a dog? The initial outlay for a puppy may not be much, especially if it is a mongrel, but the cost of equipment, food and veterinary care will soon mount up. Even the healthiest of dogs will need to see a vet at least once a year for its booster vaccinations, and it is a rare dog indeed that never falls ill. Veterinary costs are high. Consider taking out pet insurance. If you go on holiday without the dog, you will have to arrange for the dog to be cared for, such as by a house and dog sitter or in boarding kennels, and this will cost as well.

And now...

So you have thought about all the above, discussed the whole issue and you are still determined to get a new, four-footed friend. Read on!

Chapter 2 Choosing a dog

For the dog/child relationship to work out as well as possible, a lot of thought should go into the choice of breed. Dogs of every possible breed, as well as crossbreeds and mongrels, share their lives very successfully with young children, and any well-bred dog of sound temperament can make the ideal family pet. Of course, if you already own a dog and then have a baby, you may never need to address this problem. However, it cannot be denied that certain breeds of dog are more suitable as family pets than others; breeds that are renowned for their sound, easy-going tempers. Likewise, certain breeds are more suited to the experienced dog owner with no small children. Therefore, every parent who is a potential dog owner should research the subject of breeds thoroughly before making the final decision. The choice of a particular breed should never be made on looks alone, as a very cute and cuddly-looking dog may be far more demanding than a less appealing one. Dalmatians, for instance, made so popular by Disney's film *101 Dalmatians*, can make tremendous pets but they are lively and demanding dogs that require a great deal of exercise and training and, therefore, often they are not suitable for the novice owner.

CHOOSING A DOG

Pedigree or mongrel?

Many first-time dog owners opt for a mongrel or crossbred dog as opposed to a pedigree dog. It is commonly believed that mongrels are healthier than pedigrees, live longer and are more gentle in temperament. These are all fallacies! Dogs are individuals, just like people, and it is not possible to generalise as broadly as this. A mongrel may make the perfect family pet and companion for one family, but could be a disaster for another. Of course, the same is true of the pedigree dog.

First of all, forget all that you have heard about mongrels being much healthier than pedigree dogs. All dogs can fall ill, regardless of their breeding. Their stamina depends largely on their parents' stamina and their upbringing. Hereditary diseases such as hip dysplasia (which can be a crippling disease, especially in larger dogs) are no less common in mongrels than in pedigrees. It may appear that mongrels suffer less from these problems, but how many mongrels and crossbreeds are X-rayed and examined under the official health schemes? It follows that problems are discovered more frequently in pedigree dogs as the breeders become more and more diligent. Needless to say, any dog bred from two parents with bad hips is far more likely to develop hip dysplasia; the simple fact that he is a mongrel does not in any way protect him. I once owned a beautiful crossbred dog. She suffered from very severe hip dysplasia whereas my pedigree dogs have never had this problem. If you want to make as sure as you can that your dog is healthy, then purchase a puppy from parents that have been tested for hereditary diseases.

As for temperament and suitability as a pet, as mentioned earlier there are some breeds which are more suitable for families with children than others. Mongrels and crossbreeds with these breeds mixed in usually make good family pets. However, when getting a mongrel or crossbreed, especially a puppy, you are taking pot luck as to how the dog will

CHOOSING A DOG

turn out as an adult. Not knowing what breeds are involved in the mix, if two or more very different breeds are included, or which breed the puppy will resemble, you will have no idea what sort of temperament the puppy will grow up to have or even how big he will be. You may end up with a dog far bigger than you had envisaged, or far more lively and demanding more exercise than you have the time to give. Therefore, for any family with children, I would strongly recommend a pedigree dog. By buying a pedigree dog, you will have a very good idea what sort of temperament and size your puppy will have when he grows up. There are, of course, exceptions to every rule. Occasionally, a pedigree dog may exhibit a temperament quite opposite to what is usual within the breed, but this is very rare and can be avoided by purchasing your puppy from a reputable breeder.

Choosing a pedigree breed

The Kennel Club divides the various breeds of dog into seven different groups. As a general rule, the breeds within one particular group all have something in common, normally what the breed was used for originally. Therefore, gundogs were bred originally to work alongside the huntsman with the gun, toy dogs were small companion or pet dogs, and so on. Most of the breeds within one group have similar temperaments, even though size and other characteristics can vary greatly. Here follows a list of all the breeds included in each of the seven groups, together with descriptions of a selection from each group, and their suitability as pets for households with children.

Hound Group

Afghan Hound, Basenji, Basset Fauve de Bretagne, Basset Griffon Vendeen (Grand), Basset Griffon Vendeen (Petit), Basset Hound, Bavarian Mountain Hound, Beagle, Bloodhound, Borzoi, Dachshund (Longhaired), Dachshund (Miniature Longhaired), Dachshund (Smoothhaired), Dachshund (Miniature Smooth Haired), Dachshund (Wirehaired), Dachshund (Miniature Wirehaired), Deerhound, Elkhound, Finnish Spitz, Foxhound, Grand Bleu de Gascoigne, Greyhound, Hamiltonstövare, Ibizan Hound, Irish Wolfhound, Norwegian Lundehund, Otterhound, Pharaoh Hound, Rhodesian Ridgeback, Saluki, Segugio Italiano, Sloughi, Whippet.

Although there are exceptions, breeds found within the hound group are usually best avoided for first-time dog owners with children. Many hounds can be pretty stubborn and difficult to train, and they are not the sorts of breed commonly seen as pets. Exceptions include the Beagle, which can be stubborn but is a very gentle dog, good with children as he has endless patience; the Greyhound which, despite its size, does not require endless hours of exercise; and the Whippet which basically is a

CHOOSING A DOG

smaller version of the Greyhound. There are numerous ex-racing Greyhounds in dogs' homes all over the country waiting for good homes. These gentle animals can make very good pets, although often they do not mix very well with smaller animals such as cats and rabbits. The tough little Dachshund (available in two sizes and three different coat types) can also make a good pet for children although, again, being a hound he tends to have a mind of his own and is not, perhaps, the easiest of breeds to train.

Gundog Group

Bracco Italiano, Brittany, English Setter, German Shorthaired Pointer, German Wirehaired Pointer, Gordon Setter, Hungarian Vizsla, Irish Red and White Setter, Irish Setter, Italian Spinone, Kooikerhundje, Large Münsterländer, Nova Scotia Duck Tolling Retriever, Pointer, Chesapeake Bay Retriever, Curly Coated Retriever, Flat Coated Retriever, Golden Retriever, Labrador Retriever, American Cocker Spaniel, Clumber Spaniel, Cocker Spaniel, English Springer Spaniel, Field Spaniel, Irish Water Spaniel, Sussex Spaniel, Welsh Springer Spaniel, Spanish Water Dog, Weimaraner.

Dogs from the gundog group often make wonderful family pets and here we find many of the eternal favourites such as the Labrador Retriever (currently the most popular dog in the United Kingdom), the Golden Retriever and the Springer Spaniel. Most gundogs are friendly, gentle, fun-loving and patient with children. The Labrador and the Golden Retriever in particular are ideal family dogs. The various Setters are lovely pets, too, but generally these are livelier and demand more exercise, something that should be borne in mind.

The popular English Springer Spaniel, with its medium size and friendly, outgoing nature, is also an extremely energetic dog that requires a large amount of exercise and training if it is not to become bored. The smaller Cocker Spaniel is always popular, but over-breeding by unscrupulous breeders has meant that, sadly, these days Cockers frequently suffer from temperament problems, showing serious aggression. If you are considering buying a Cocker Spaniel, take extra care to ensure that the pup comes from parents of very sound temperament.

Some of the more unusual gundogs, such as the German Pointer and the Weimaraner, can be excellent dogs with children. However these breeds are rather tougher and more demanding than the Spaniels/Setters/Retrievers so are, perhaps, best avoided by the novice.

CHOOSING A DOG

Terrier Group
Airedale Terrier, Australian Terrier, Bedlington Terrier, Border Terrier, Bull Terrier, Bull Terrier (Miniature), Cairn Terrier, Cesky Terrier, Dandie Dinmont Terrier, Fox Terrier (Smooth), Fox Terrier (Wire), Glen of Imaal Terrier, Irish Terrier, Kerry Blue Terrier, Lakeland Terrier, Manchester Terrier, Norfolk Terrier, Norwich Terrier, Parson Jack Russell Terrier, Scottish Terrier, Sealyham Terrier, Skye Terrier, Soft Coated Wheaten Terrier, Staffordshire Bull Terrier, Welsh Terrier, West Highland White Terrier.

Whether or not terriers make good pets for children is a subject that will always be hotly debated. Terriers (with a few exceptions such as the Airedale, which is known as the King of terriers, and the Soft Coated Wheaten) are generally small dogs with a big attitude. Terriers are forward, tough and hardly frightened of anything. As such, they can tolerate being handled by children, put up with with endless games of rough and tumble, and do not mind going for long walks even in bad weather. At the same time, they can be short-tempered and prone to snap. Whether a particular breed of terrier will make the ideal pet for your family is something that you ought to discuss in more detail with some terrier breeders and owners. Generally, though, it can be said that popular terrier breeds such as the West Highland White Terrier (Westie), the Cairn, Parson Jack Russell (which is the long-legged version of the breed, the only one recognised by The Kennel Club), and the Welsh Terrier are best kept by families with children of ten years and upwards who are old enough to understand that they must not be too rough with the dog or he may feel the need to defend himself.

CHOOSING A DOG

Utility Group
Boston Terrier, Bulldog, Canaan Dog, Chow Chow, Dalmatian, French Bulldog, German Spitz (Klein), German Spitz (Mittel), Japanese Akita, Japanese Shiba Inu, Japanese Spitz, Keeshond, Lhasa Apso, Mexican Hairless Dog, Miniature Schnauzer, Poodle (Standard), Poodle (Miniature), Poodle (Toy), Schipperke, Schnauzer, Shar Pei, Shih Tzu, Tibetan Spaniel, Tibetan Terrier.

The utility breeds are those dogs which do not fit into any other category. Therefore, this group shows very varied breeds, and no generalisation can be made about them. The breed from this group that perhaps most children will ask for is the Dalmatian. The Dalmatian is a lovely dog that can be excellent as a family pet, but it is a large breed that demands a great deal of exercise and lots of training so that it does not get out of hand. The Poodle (three different sizes) will make an excellent pet for most families, as long as it is understood that this intelligent animal needs a lot of professional grooming. Likewise, for those not put off by the prospect of daily coat care, the Tibetan Spaniel, the Tibetan Terrier and the Lhasa Apso are friendly, smaller breeds that normally have very good temperaments.

Toy Group
Affenpinscher, Australian Silky Terrier, Bichon Frisé, Bolognese, Cavalier King Charles Spaniel, Chihuahua (Long Coat), Chihuahua (Smooth Coat), Chinese Crested, Coton de Tulear, English Toy Terrier (Black and Tan), Griffon Bruxellois, Havanese, Italian Greyhound, Japanese Chin, King Charles Spaniel, Löwchen, Maltese, Miniature Pinscher, Papillon, Pekingese, Pomeranian, Pug, Yorkshire Terrier.

The toy breeds are the smallest of all breeds, with the Chihuahua being the smallest breed of dog in the world. Toy dogs are all bred for one purpose only: to be pets and companions (as well show dogs). Often they have very good temperaments and make lovely pets. However, toy breeds can be very small indeed, and may not be a good idea for the family with very young children. A very small dog can be picked up and carried around by even a one or two-year-old child and, if dropped, may break a leg or worse. Also, toddlers may fall over the dog or on top of it, with disastrous consequences for the dog. Such smaller breeds are more suitable for older children who know how to handle dogs with care.

CHOOSING A DOG

CHOOSING A DOG

The Yorkshire Terrier is a very popular little dog within this group but, again, it is very small and not ideal for very young children. Also it has a long coat that needs daily care and, sometimes a fierce Terrier temperament! Without a doubt, experts agree that the Cavalier King Charles Spaniel is one of the best breeds for families with children of all ages. The Cavalier (which is slightly different from its rarer cousin, the King Charles Spaniel), is the largest of the toy breeds. Cavaliers are happy, outgoing, friendly dogs with a wonderful nature. They are large enough not to be picked up by small children, yet not too big for a child to walk on a lead (under supervision, of course). They are happy to go for long walks, but don't mind staying at home in front of the fire if the weather is bad.

Pastoral Group

Anatolian Shepherd Dog, Australian Cattle Dog, Australian Shepherd Dog, Bearded Collie, Bergamasco, Border Collie, Briard, Rough Collie, Smooth Collie, Estrela Mountain Dog, Finnish Lapphund, German Shepherd Dog (Alsatian), Hovawart, Hungarian Kuvasz, Hungarian Puli, Komondor, Lancashire Heeler, Maremma Sheepdog, Pyrenean Mountain Dog, Pyrenean Sheepdog, Samoyed, Shetland Sheepdog, Swedish Lapphund, Swedish Vallhund, Welsh Corgi (Cardigan), Welsh Corgi (Pembroke).

The pastoral group consists of dog breeds that were used as sheep or cattledogs. These days, several of the breeds are kept only as pets and not as working dogs, such as the Shetland Sheepdog (commonly known as the Sheltie, the miniature version of the classic Rough Collie), the Bearded Collie, the Old English Sheepdog and the Corgi. They are

CHOOSING A DOG

suitable as pets, but it is important that any prospective owners looks carefully into each breed's particular needs with regard to coat care. The Bearded Collie and Old English Sheepdog are friendly, beautiful dogs, but they have a large amount of coat and need daily grooming. In wet weather, after a walk, they are sure to bring in mud.

Other breeds are still used for their original purpose, in particular the Border Collie. Border Collies are very popular pet dogs and can be marvellous companions, but I would advise anyone to think carefully before acquiring one. This most intelligent of breeds needs an enormous amount of exercise and training to be able to live a happy, fulfilled life. A bored Border Collie is like a demolition team! The Collies that you see on 'One Man and His Dog' or in the obedience or agility competitions at Crufts are highly-trained dogs; they do not exhibit behaviour that will come naturally without training. Also remember that, as a herding dog, the Collie often will want to 'round up his flock' and, if there is only a human one available, he may attempt to round up the children. A Collie herding sheep will nip at their heels to get them moving, and a pet Collie may have the same tendencies. This does not mean that the breed is aggressive, but young children may mistake this behaviour for aggression, and many a Collie has been handed in to rescue for the reason that 'he nips the children'.

The German Shepherd Dog (Alsatian) is another breed that makes a marvellous companion and guard dog, but **only** if carefully trained, and this breed needs more training than many other breeds. Think carefully before making your choice if you are considering a Pastoral breed.

Working Group
Alaskan Malamute, Beauceron, Bernese Mountain Dog, Bouvier Des Flandres, Boxer, Bullmastiff, Continental Landseer, Dobermann, Eskimo Dog, Giant Schnauzer, Great Dane, Leonberger, Mastiff, Neapolitan Mastiff, Newfoundland, Pinscher, Portuguese Water Dog, Rottweiler, St Bernard, Siberian Husky, Tibetan Mastiff

Working dogs were bred for a specific purpose, for example to act as guard dogs or sled dogs. Very few of these breeds will make suitable pets for the novice owner. Several are giant in size, such as the St Bernard, the Great Dane and the Newfoundland. Although dogs with excellent temperaments, their sheer size makes them unsuitable for many families. It doesn't necessarily follow that any giant breed will need hours of exercise every day. The St Bernard and the Newfoundland, for example, are quite content with short walks as opposed to miles of exercise. But their size makes them unsuitable as pets unless you have

CHOOSING A DOG

a large house, and it is important to remember that giant breeds need extra careful feeding and care, as they are more prone to skeletal problems as they grow than smaller breeds.

Other working breeds, such as the Rottweiler and the Dobermann, are widely used as guard dogs, and to a certain extent have a bad reputation. Both these breeds can make excellent pets and they are not less trustworthy than other breeds. **But,** this is provided that the dog is bought from a reputable breeder who only breeds from dogs with the soundest temperament, and that the dog is well trained and exercised. It is probably better to avoid these breeds, particularly with young children around.

The Boxer is a very friendly dog who usually loves children, but he is very boisterous, slobbers a lot and needs a great deal of exercise. These are important factors to bear in mind when making your choice. Breeds such as the Alaskan Malamute or the Siberian Husky are still used as sled dogs, and these specialist breeds do not really make suitable family pets for the novice dog owner.

Chapter 3 Where to buy your dog

Acquiring a dog is a major undertaking, as he will be part of your family for the next 10–15 years. Never buy on impulse simply because a particular puppy is very cute, or because you feel sorry for it. Considering the amount of time the dog is going to spend with you and your family, it is well worth the effort to take some extra time looking for the dog that is right for you, even if this means having to wait a few months longer than you had planned originally.

Puppy farms and superstores

The first rule to remember is that a puppy should never be bought from a pet shop, puppy superstore or dealer. It is fair to say that most reputable pet shops do not offer puppies or kittens for sale. It may seem convenient to visit a 'puppy supermarket' where you can view puppies of different breeds, pay your money and take your pick. The offer of a guarantee and Kennel Club registration papers also are reassuring. However, puppies sold from these outlets are usually bred at puppy farms. The bitches at these farms are kept for one purpose only: to produce as many puppies as possible which the owner can sell for a large profit. Bitches are bred at every season and when they are too old or too exhausted to produce more puppies, they are discarded or put to sleep. Many are kept in appalling conditions and no consideration is given to their health and temperament. Sadly, The Kennel Club still registers puppies from such establishments, but this registration is no guarantee of a well-bred pup.

Many puppies sold from pet shops suffer from health and temperament problems, and many do not live to see their first birthday. Those that do often cost their owners far more than a puppy obtained from a reputable breeder would have done, as the vet's fees soon mount up. Often the actual purchase price is higher than that charged by recognised breeders. Quite apart from the way in which he was bred, a puppy sold from a pet shop will have been through a lot of unnecessary stress. In order to be available at the age of eight weeks, when most puppies are bought, he will have been taken from his mother at an early age, transported (frequently a long way, as most puppy farms are located in Wales), and then put on view in a pet shop where he will be exposed to all sorts of health risks. Compare this to a puppy bought directly from the breeder: he will leave his mother at eight weeks of age and travel direct to your home. It is very easy to fall for the sad-looking puppy in the pet shop window and buy him simply because you feel sorry for him but, by doing so, you are encouraging the puppy farmer to continue. If nobody bought these puppies, the demand would cease and the dealers would be forced out of business.

Breeders

A reputable breeder will be able to show you the puppies' mother, and she will be your best guide as to how the puppies will turn out as adults. Never buy a puppy if the mother shows any signs of aggression or nervousness. The reputable breeder will answer any questions that you may have – and you should have plenty! He or she will also ask you a number of questions before even considering selling you a puppy. Avoid breeders who appear more interested in your money than the home you are able to offer the dog. A

WHERE TO BUY YOUR DOG

caring breeder wants to make sure that all his or her puppies go to good homes, and so will want all the details about you and your family. The questions will include, for example, have you ever owned a dog before, what made you decide on the breed in question, how you live, are you aware of the responsibilities involved in looking after a puppy and so on. This is not prying, this is simply being a good breeder. A reputable breeder will also be able to show you certificates proving that their breeding animals have been tested clear of hereditary diseases (exactly what diseases depends on the breed. Read up on the breed beforehand, and do ask The Kennel Club for advice). The breeder will not deliver any puppy to you, but will want to see you in their home. You will receive a pedigree, KC-registration certificate, diet sheet, worming certificate and, possibly, insurance that will cover the puppy for a limited period. Never accept anything less than this for a puppy sold as a pedigree.

Most of these breeders breed dogs as a hobby, not as a main source of income. It is very difficult, not to say impossible, to make money out of breeding dogs without cutting corners, so it follows that most caring breeders make little or no profit from their hobby. A breeder who offers several (probably of the most popular) breeds for sale should be viewed with suspicion as most hobby breeders concentrate on just one or two breeds.

The Kennel Club can supply you with a list of breeders of your chosen breed. Contact The Kennel Club (1–5 Clarges Street, London W1Y 8AB) and you will be sent free of charge a puppy pack that will include much of the information you need as a prospective

WHERE TO BUY YOUR DOG

puppy buyer. The Kennel Club can also give you details about breed clubs, which are your best source of information about how to find a good breeder in your area. There are national and regional clubs for most breeds, and the committee members usually are only too willing to put you in touch with good breeders. Some may have lists of puppies currently for sale.

Rescue Dogs

There are thousands of unwanted dogs at any one time desperately looking for good homes. Rescue centres such as the Royal Society for the Prevention of Cruelty to Animals (RSPCA) mainly re-home mongrels and crossbreeds but it is not unusual for pedigree dogs to end up in these places as well. If you have decided on a particular breed of dog, you can do a good deed by giving a home to a rescued dog. However, it is important to realise that a rescued dog, particularly if adult, has a possibly unknown background and may have had bad experiences. Always carefully assess the temperament of any rescue dog before taking it on, and discuss any dog with the staff at the centre. If you are interested in one particular breed, the breed club will be able to give details about their breed rescue service. This is operated by unpaid volunteers for the love of their breed. For popular breeds, there may be a breed rescue for every region of the country.

The dogs that end up in breed rescue usually do so for the same reasons that dogs end up in general rescue; their owners may have grown tired of them or were unable to cope for one reason or another (divorce, emigration and so on). Each dog that is taken in will

WHERE TO BUY YOUR DOG

be carefully assessed and, as the numbers are much smaller than in general rescue, more care can be taken to find the right home for the right dog. All rescue organisations will want to question you carefully before rehoming a dog to you, and they will probably want to do a home check as well. Rescue dogs are not given away; rescue centres could not survive without donations or contributions and also they do not want people to think they can get a pedigree dog for free.

Puppy or adult dog?

Most people will want to buy a puppy as opposed to an adult dog, which is perfectly understandable. You will be able to train a puppy yourself and he will fit in easily with his new family. An adult dog may come with acquired bad habits and he may take longer to settle into a new home. Most rescue dogs are adults (although puppies, particularly mongrels, are not unusual), and if you have decided on giving a home to a rescued dog, you may not have the choice of a puppy. It is probably fair to say that for the average first-time dog-owning family, it is easier if a puppy is bought. However, a puppy needs to be house-trained, wants food four times a day and has to be given some general training. All this takes much time and patience. Nor can a small puppy be left alone at all until he is older. Therefore, an adult dog may be the easier option, as long as you have made sure that he has a good temperament and no bad habits that you will not be able to cope with, such as excessive barking, pulling on the lead, and so on.

Some breeders 'run on' several puppies from a litter until they are 4–6 months or even older before they decide which one to keep for themselves for showing. You may be able to buy an older puppy from a breeder but you should check what sort of life the puppy has had. If he has spent all his life in kennels with little or no contact with outside life, then it may be best not to buy him if you are unused to dogs. Early socialisation (for example, getting used to people, traffic, household noises such as the television and vacuum cleaner) is essential for puppies, and a six-month-old pup that has spent all his life in an outside kennel will have lost out on all this and may find it hard to cope.

Ideally, a puppy should not be younger than eight weeks. This is the age when most reputable breeders let their puppies go to new homes as by this age they are fully weaned and ready to leave their mother and littermates.

Dog or Bitch?

Whether you choose a dog or a bitch is very much a matter of personal choice. Most dog owners have their particular preference. Both sexes can make equally good pets and gender need not be a big consideration when choosing your puppy. Dogs (males) usually grow slightly larger than bitches (females). Unless they are neutered (spayed), bitches come into season twice a year. It is not true that bitches are always gentler and easier to train than dogs, far from it. Neither is it true that un-neutered dogs are always prone to stray and roam the streets. Different dogs behave in different ways. The way you treat and train your dog will have much more effect on behaviour than the sex.

A word here on neutering. It is often said that to be a responsible dog owner you have to have your pet neutered to prevent unwanted puppies. I believe that if your pet is properly looked after (the dog or bitch is well trained and not allowed to stray), then no unwanted puppies will result. Also, it is not always true that neutering will automatically improve

WHERE TO BUY YOUR DOG

temperament or reduce aggression. Again, training and upbringing are what matter. Many owners feel that they must spay their bitches as it can be very inconvenient and messy when she comes into season and bleeds for three weeks, must be kept away from dogs and so on. Remember that neutering is a major, albeit routine, operation. If you want to avoid the hassle of a bitch in season, the easiest option is to choose a dog instead. There are plenty of arguments both for and against routine neutering so I would advise you discuss this with your puppy's breeder before coming to a decision. He or she will have a great deal of experience with the breed and is better placed to advise you than anyone else.

Selecting your puppy

Finally the day has come for you and your family to choose the dog of your dreams. If you are lucky, you could find yourselves with an entire litter of adorable puppies from which to choose. More commonly though, the breeder will show you perhaps two or three puppies as some may have been booked already. It is not uncommon that just a single puppy is left for sale. But whether you have several puppies to choose from or just the one, you should still take your time and examine him carefully to make sure that he is the right one for you.

Health, of course, is of utmost importance. Examine the puppy for obvious signs of ill-health such as runny eyes, a dirty tail area (which might indicate diarrhoea), and signs of fleas in the coat. A healthy puppy will have bright, clear eyes and a nose which may be either cold or warm but not crusty. There should be no discharge from the nose, other than possibly a perfectly clear, watery fluid which some puppies have.

WHERE TO BUY YOUR DOG

WHERE TO BUY YOUR DOG

The ears should smell clean and the coat should be reasonably clean and certainly free from fleas. Puppies have an incredible knack for getting dirty so I wouldn't worry too much about a bit of dirt as long as the puppy looks well. Signs of fleas include flea dirt in the coat that can be seen as small black specks, particularly easy to see on a light-coloured animal. If rubbed between wet fingers, this will turn red. The healthy young puppy will have a firm body which often is quite rounded, but a distended stomach and a prominent backbone could indicate worms.

Temperament is just as important as health, and the best indication you can get of a puppy's future temperament is to meet his mother. Do not accept any excuses why the mother may not be around and never buy a puppy unless you see the mother. A puppy dealer might pose as the actual breeder of the litter when in fact it was purchased from another source.

Years ago, it used to be said that you should always choose the bold puppy that immediately runs up to greet you, and never the shy one that sits in the corner. This is partly true, as the first puppy to greet you probably will be the boldest one and the quiet one may be a bit nervous. However, consider yourself and your family and try to match your temperament with the puppy's. If you are a loud, outgoing family then by all means choose that bold puppy. He will need a firm hand in training but will be able to put up with the hustle and bustle of your family life which may be a bit much for the quieter puppy. If, on the other hand, you have a much quieter manner and your children are calm, then the less adventurous puppy will be a more suitable choice. For most people, though, the middle-of-the-road puppy, the one that neither greets you first nor last, will be the best choice. If you are unsure, ask the breeder who will have had plenty of experience in matching the right puppy to the right owner.

Chapter 4 Your new pup at home

Bringing home your new dog

Before bringing home your new pet, whether puppy or adult, you should have made your preparations. You should have bought all the dog's equipment (bed, food and water bowls, toys, collar and lead) and put them in place. Very importantly, you need to have prepared your children about what to expect from the new family member and how to behave with him.

Like young children, puppies need a great deal of sleep. Children must be taught to leave the puppy alone when he is sleeping. The puppy's bed should be his den, where he can rest undisturbed. An eight-week-old puppy sleeps during large parts of the day, so children must understand that he is too young to be involved in too many games and certainly too young to be taken for walks. However, puppies grow quickly and before long he will be old enough to join in fully with all the fun.

The children must also be taught to leave the dog alone when he is eating. A well-trained dog should allow anyone to remove his food even whilst he is eating it, but a puppy will not yet have learned this lesson. The same is even more true for an adult rescue dog whose background you may not know. Never allow the children to touch the dog while he is eating or he may snap at them.

Children of all ages seem to leave toys, games and clothes strewn all around the house. A new puppy will not be able to tell the difference between his toys, made for chewing, and your child's favourite teddy or expensive trainers, which definitely must not be chewed. Impress upon the children that their possessions must be kept out of the way when the puppy is around so that they do not get chewed. It will not be the puppy's fault if a toy is ruined accidentally and he should not be punished for this. In addition, a small puppy may become ill if he chews and swallows pieces of plastic toy.

It is good idea to invest in either a child gate or special dog gate (same construction but stronger and taller) so that the dog can be shut away safely in one room, such as the kitchen, when the children have their belongings out. This way, he will be able to see what is going on, and the children will be able to watch him, but they will not be able to interfere with each other. Alternatively, buy a large dog crate where the dog can be locked away for peace and quiet. As long as the crate is large enough, has comfortable bedding and some toys, is introduced to the dog as his special place and is never used as a place of punishment, the dog will use this happily as his den. This is particularly suitable during the night and when family members leave the

YOUR NEW PUP AT HOME

house, as you will know that the dog is in a safe place where he cannot do any damage or come to any harm.

When arriving home with the new pet, first allow him to wander around the house, having a good sniff and look at everything. Show him where everything important is, such as his bed, water bowl and the back door. Do not let the children interfere too much at this stage as the dog will be feeling a little insecure in these new surroundings and needs a chance to get settled in properly before he is ready for games and cuddles. There will be plenty of time for that later on.

The first night

Any puppy is bound to feel lonely at first, having just been separated from his mother and littermates. This will be particularly evident during the first night. You have to start as you mean to go on and, even on that first night, the puppy should be made to sleep where you want him to spend his nights in the future. It is very tempting to allow a young pup to sleep in your bedroom during those first restless nights, and the children are bound to plead to be allowed to have the puppy in bed with them. If you start by allowing the puppy in the bedrooms, he will take this as the norm and the habit will be hard to break later on. Also the dog should be at the bottom of the 'pack' (your family) and so should not be allowed to sleep with the rest of the family. In fact, he should not be allowed upstairs at all.

When you go to bed on that first night, do not make a big deal out of it. Simply make sure that the puppy is well fed, has been outside, has some toys and somewhere comfortable to sleep,

YOUR NEW PUP AT HOME

YOUR NEW PUP AT HOME

turn out the lights and leave him alone. It is best if the puppy does not have access to more than one room (ideally the kitchen or another room which has a floor that is easy to clean), as inevitably there will be accidents during the night.

More often than not, eventually the puppy will start to cry when he realises that he is all alone. Do not give in to the the temptation to go in to reassure him as this will teach him that making a lot of noise will make his owners appear. Simply talk to the puppy through the closed door telling him firmly but kindly to be quiet, then leave again. That very first

YOUR NEW PUP AT HOME

night you will probably be disturbed a few times, but after this the puppy will start to get used to being on his own and will accept it as the norm. With a particularly restless puppy, there are some tried and tested tricks that you can try. A hot-water-bottle for warmth and a ticking clock under a blanket to remind him of his mother's heartbeat, may help him settle down. A cuddly toy may help, but make sure no small parts such as bead eyes or nose can be chewed off and swallowed. An old blanket or item of clothing with some familiar smell on it (such as a blanket used at the breeder's house or that someone in the family has slept on for a day or two) can also do the trick.

Going to the vet
After a couple of days your new pet will begin to settle down and get used to his new routine. This is when it is time to take him to the vet for his very first vaccination and check-up. At this time the puppy should also start a course of worming treatment. More information on health is in chapter 6.

Take care
One thing you must never forget is that no dog, however trustworthy, should be left alone with a young child. You may trust your dog, but are you completely sure that your three-year-old won't poke a pencil inside the dog's ear, just to see what happens? Most attacks on children by dogs are provoked in some way or another. Always be safe rather than sorry.

Chapter 5 Your dog and a new baby

Toxocariasis

When I was pregnant with my first child, the visiting midwife looked disapprovingly at my collection of dogs, cats and other animals and told me firmly that 'animals and children do not mix!'. Sadly, it is this sort of attitude that makes large numbers of women feel that they have to give up their dog simply because they are pregnant. Expectant mothers are told horror stories about dogs becoming so jealous of the new baby that eventually they attack it. Not to mention all the media warnings about dog mess causing blindness in children.

Let me put your mind at rest. If you prepare your dog properly, he will welcome the new baby almost as much as you will. Regardless of breed, your dog can easily become the baby's faithful companion as well as yours. As for blindness, the roundworm *Toxocara canis* can, in rare instances, cause damaged eyesight in children and adults through a disease known as Toxocariasis. Television and newspapers frequently report that hundreds of children are blinded by this each year. The truth is somewhat different. *Toxocara canis* can cause Toxocariasis only if the worm's eggs, found in the dog's faeces, are left in the faeces on the ground for two weeks, allowing the eggs to develop into larvae. These then have to be eaten for them to get inside the human body. Only then can Toxocariasis develop. Even then, damaged eyesight is rare and, at worst, partial blindness in one eye may be the outcome. No case of total blindness caused by Toxocariasis in a human has been reported. The precautions are simple:

1. Worm your dog regularly, preferably every three months, with tablets supplied by your vet as usually these are far more effective than over-the-counter worming tablets.
2. Clear up any dog mess every day from your garden and dispose of it. Also clear up any mess that your dog makes when you are out. The Toxocara eggs will then never have the chance to develop into larvae.
3. Never allow children to play near dog mess and teach them to wash their hands after each game with a dog.

Preparing for the new baby

So how do you successfully introduce a new baby to a dog that you may have had for several years? The key is always to treat the dog as a dog, not as a human, and to start preparations before the baby is born. It is all based on how dogs would behave in a pack in the wild.

Sleeping arrangements

First of all, if your dog is allowed in the bedroom, or anywhere upstairs, you should gradually get him used to the fact that this is no longer acceptable. You have nine months in which to do it, so there is no rush.

If your dog sleeps in your bedroom, start by gradually moving his bed away. This can be a very gradual process, with the bed first being moved to the far side of the bedroom, then to the other side of the open bedroom door, then outside the closed bedroom door, then further away and, finally, downstairs. Do not make a big deal out of the move, and do not treat the dog as though you feel sorry for him as dogs quickly pick up on human emotions. Simply present him with the fact that his bed is being moved, and he will accept this. Similarly, do not allow your dog upstairs. The easiest way to achieve this is to fit a stairgate at the top and bottom of the stairs. You will need these anyway for when your baby becomes a toddler and starts to walk.

Playing with your dog
The next step is to get your dog used to not having constant attention. He will have to learn that no longer will he be the most important factor in your life. Do not allow him to walk up to you and demand a fuss. If he comes asking to be stroked or played with, ignore him. Once he has left, wait a few moments, then call him over, play and make a fuss of him. Then say 'off' or 'enough' or whatever command you prefer, and ignore him again. The idea is to teach the dog that he will only get your attention when you say so, that he himself cannot dictate this. This is very important as soon you will have your hands full with the new baby, and you will not be able to start playing with the dog when you are in the middle of a nappy change or comforting a colicky baby.

Vary exercise times
It will also be a good idea if you get your dog used to not always having his daily walk at the same time because you will no longer be able to guarantee that you can get out at the same time each day. If possible, find somebody who can walk the dog for you sometimes, as you will feel less inclined to go for long walks as your pregnancy advances. It is also a good idea to buy your baby's pram or pushchair well in advance, and buy a model with as large wheels as possible. Then you will be able to walk over grass and rough terrain with the pushchair, which I promise is virtually impossible with a pushchair with small wheels! If you start practising before the baby is born, you can teach your dog to walk calmly at the side of the pushchair without pulling on the lead.

YOUR DOG AND A NEW BABY

Feeding and taking things away

When feeding your dog, always feed him after the human members of the family have eaten. As packleaders, you are entitled to eat first, and to get the best bits. Never give the dog titbits at the table. Also teach him that you are allowed to take things from him, even food. You can practise this both with toys and with his food bowl. Give your dog a toy, then gently take it out of his mouth, saying 'give'. Praise him when he lets go and return the toy. Do the same with his food. Teach your dog to wait until he is allowed to start eating. Put the food bowl on the floor in front of him, hold his collar and say 'wait' before giving a command such as 'okay' and allowing him to touch the food. He will soon learn to wait. You can then start to take his bowl away during the meal. Any good-natured dog should accept this. Always praise him for allowing you to take his food and always give it back again. This is very important as young children often try to take objects from dogs and the dog must know that he is to allow anybody to take anything from him at any time, however much he wants to keep it.

The day baby comes home

Once the day has come for you to bring home your new baby, try not to make a too big deal out of the event. Keep everything as calm and normal as possible. On arriving home, greet your dog as usual and allow him to sniff the baby. Praise him for doing so calmly. Then tell him 'enough' and ignore him. The important fact is to realise that your dog is not human and must not be ascribed human emotions. The dog will not feel 'jealous' of the new baby as long as you have already taught him that he cannot have your undivided attention whenever he feels like it.

New parents frequently make the mistake of trying to reassure the dog, making a big fuss of him so that he doesn't 'feel left out'. This is a very serious mistake, and one that can be dangerous. If you pay your dog a lot of extra attention, thinking that otherwise he will feel jealous of the baby, in effect you are telling him that he is more important than the baby. Then he might feel it his right to 'reprimand' the baby, that is, attack. After all, his pack leaders clearly have told him that he ranks above the baby so surely it is up to him to put the baby in its place? This is how accidents happen. To ensure that your dog treats the new baby with enthusiasm, show him clearly that the baby is far more important than he is. Make a fuss of the baby, not of the dog. Only make a fuss of the dog when you decide it is time. Talk to and cuddle your baby in front of the dog. He will watch with interest as he is being ignored by you and will realise that this new human, although tiny, must be very important indeed and certainly ranks higher than he does. If you follow this simple rule, then the dog will treat the baby with the same respect as he treats you, as his superior.

Dogs need packleaders, it is what they would be used to if they were in the wild and a dog that is not firmly (but kindly) treated and knows his place in the pack will only be confused. A dog that knows his place will feel secure and happy. I can guarantee that it will not take long before you notice that the dog becomes protective towards the baby, carefully monitoring any visitors that want to hold it. In fact, you may have to keep a close eye on the dog when the midwife and health visitor call during the first weeks after the baby's birth, as the dog may regard them as intruders wishing to harm the baby. You will have to tell the dog that as long as you say so other people are allowed to touch the baby.

The toddler
Once the baby becomes a toddler and starts to walk, you will have to keep a close eye on the two of them. More than likely, your dog will be very patient with your child. My own dogs put up with everything from having their teeth inspected to small fingers poked inside their noses and their tails pulled. Nevertheless, I would never leave a dog and child alone together. A hurt or startled dog may snap out of fear and pain. For example, a barely-mobile child might fall on top of an elderly, arthritic dog or poke his fingers into the dog's eyes. As soon as my own children were old enough to grasp the concept, my husband and I showed them the difference between a living animal and a toy by allowing a toy animal to be thrown about, hit and squeezed, telling them this is all right. However with a real animal, we stressed, you must always be careful or he will get hurt.

In conclusion
With a bit of common sense, the relationship between child and dog should become one that is almost second to none. Living as I do with two small children and seven dogs, I know what a close bond a child and dog can form.

CARE AND EQUIPMENT

Chapter 6 Care and equipment

Health care

As mentioned earlier, after your new dog has had a couple of days to settle in with you, take him to the veterinary surgeon for vaccinations and a check-up. Puppies are usually vaccinated at the ages of 8 and 12 weeks, and then need a booster injection every year. This is essential, as vaccination protects against potentially fatal diseases. The diseases normally vaccinated against are Distemper, Leptospirosis, Hepatitis and Parvovirus. It is also possible to vaccinate against Kennel Cough, which may be worth considering especially if your dog meets many other dogs. Discuss this with your vet.

Worming is another essential exercise, and all dogs should be wormed regularly for both roundworm and tapeworm. Your vet will be able to sell you tablets that kill off both types of worm in a single dose, and these tablets are far more effective than any over-the-counter alternatives.

Most dogs will catch fleas at some point in their lives but nowadays it is very easy to eradicate fleas totally. Forget all the hassle with flea collars, conventional sprays and medicated shampoos. Your vet will be able to supply you with flea treatment either in tablet form, as a liquid put onto the dog's neck, or as a spray far more effective than the old kind of flea spray. All these treatments will leave your dog free of fleas for several months. Again, any flea treatment supplied by your vet is more effective than over-the-counter remedies.

As long as your dog is kept up-to-date with his vaccinations, is wormed regularly and treated for fleas, has a good diet, grooming and exercise, he should stay healthy. Obviously, dogs can fall ill just like people can, and you should always see a vet at the first sign of trouble. It is wise to take out health insurance for your dog, as this will cover most of the veterinary costs should your dog succumb to a serious or long-term illness, or have an accident.

Feeding

A good diet is essential for your dog's well being. With the vast array of different dog foods available, in canned or dry form, it can be extremely difficult for the new owner to know what to give. Your first option should always be to ask the dog's breeders what they recommend, as they will have many years' experience of feeding to attain maximum condition. If your dog is a rescue, or you want a second opinion, ask your vet for advice.

Young puppies from approximately eight weeks of age up to 4–5 months will need four meals a day. Initially, one of these should be a milk meal (for example, milk and cereal). At 4–5 months, the number of feeds can be dropped to three and, at about 8–9 months, two meals will be sufficient. Small breeds mature more

CARE AND EQUIPMENT

quickly than larger ones and can be fed as adults earlier. For growing puppies (a dog is classified as a puppy until its first birthday) special puppy foods are available that contain all the extra vitamins and minerals needed. I recommend that an adult dog is fed twice a day, as giving just one meal can cause certain problems, such as gastric torsion (twisted gut), especially in the larger breeds.

Do not give your dog treats between meals, other than the occasional chew. Teach your children not to let the dog have their leftover food or to give him/her titbits from the table, and the dog will never start to beg for food. It can be very annoying to have a large dog sitting next to the dinner table drooling in anticipation of food. If he is never used to titbits, this will never occur. It's as simple as that.

Exercise

All dogs need exercise, regardless of breed, but how much depends on the age and breed of the dog. As mentioned in chapter 2, different breeds can have very different exercise requirements. A Springer Spaniel, for instance, would not be happy with any less than an hour's good run every day, whereas many toy or giant breeds are quite content with half an hour's more sedate walk. Research your breed's requirements properly so that you know what is needed.

CARE AND EQUIPMENT

Puppies should only go for very short walks until they are older. This is particularly important to remember for the larger breeds. If a Labrador puppy, for instance, is taken out for long walks from an early age, his bones will not develop properly and he may even develop hip dysplasia as a result. Always allow a puppy to exercise at his own pace. Do not let younger children take the dog for a walk by themselves. It is highly likely that both children and pup will get over-excited and play too strenuously. Also, do not let your children drag him around on a lead expecting him to follow, as this is too strenuous for a young dog.

You can begin to take your dog for proper walks from the age of six months and then gradually increase the length of the daily walk. Large breeds (Labrador size and upwards) are not fully developed until they are 18 months old and, until then, the dog should not be allowed too much exercise. That is not to say that he should be denied exercise. That would be very unfair and would cause problems because the dog would not be able to get used to the experience of a walk. Always use your common sense and allow your puppy to set the pace whenever possible.

Grooming

The amount of grooming that your dog will require depends entirely upon what sort of coat he has so it is important to look into the requirements of the individual breeds before making your final choice. For instance, a smooth-coated breed such as the Boxer will need minimal coat care, the occasional going over with a rubber brush sufficing. For a shorthaired dog such as a Labrador, a weekly brushing with a bristle brush should do nicely. The amount of grooming will need to be increased when he is in moult, as he will then shed more hair than usual.

Wire-coated breeds, such as Wirehaired Dachshunds and many terriers, need professional hand-stripping two or three times a year. This entails the removal of all old, dead hair by hand. It is possible to learn how to do this yourself, but the pet dog owner may find it easier to leave it to the professional dog groomer or, perhaps, the dog's

CARE AND EQUIPMENT

breeder if he or she offers this service. Naturally, all this will involve further expense.

Between the professional grooming sessions you will need to comb the wirehaired dog with a metal comb a couple of times a week at least. A bristle brush will also be a good help. Longhaired breeds such as Golden Retrievers and Irish Setters require combing and brushing at least once a week, preferably more. Really longhaired breeds, such as Old English Sheepdogs, Rough Collies and Shih Tzus, need a daily grooming session to keep their coat free of knots and tangles. Never neglect the grooming of such a breed, as the fur quickly gets matted. Most Spaniel breeds need professional clipping approximately every four months, as their fur will grow too long and will be difficult to keep groomed properly. In between seeing the groomer, at least two weekly grooming sessions with a bristle brush and metal comb are needed. Breeds that do not shed fur, in particular the Poodle and the Bichon Frisé, have very dense fur that mats easily. These dogs need daily grooming, and clipping at the grooming parlour every six weeks to look their best. Again, if neglected, their coats will become seriously matted, which will cause the dog a lot of discomfort.

When grooming your dog, always take the opportunity to check him over carefully. Look to see that the ears are clean and free of discharge, and do not smell bad. Check the eyes for any sign of discharge. Examine the claws – dogs that are exercised on soft ground usually need their nails trimmed; how frequently will depend on the individual dog's nail growth. Also check the dog's skin for any signs of redness, sores or fleas.

Do not forget to inspect the teeth. From 2–3 years of age, most dogs will start to develop tartar on their teeth, which needs to be removed. You can do this yourself using a dentist's toothscraper, or you can prevent tartar appearing by brushing your dog's teeth regularly. Special doggie toothbrushes and meat-flavoured toothpaste are available from pet shops and veterinary surgeries. If your dog's teeth become severely affected by tartar, the vet will have to de-scale them which will involve anaesthetising the dog.

Most dogs need the occasional bath. Small breeds can be bathed in the kitchen sink, using a shower brush attachment slipped onto the tap, or you can bath your dog in your own bath, making sure to put down a non-slip rubber mat first. Always use special dog shampoos, never human ones as these can be harmful to dogs. Take care not to get any water or shampoo inside the dog's ears, nose or eyes, and rinse out every trace of shampoo. Then towel dry vigorously and do not allow your dog out until he is perfectly dry. Do not bath your dog too frequently as this will remove the natural oils from the coat and skin which may cause skin problems. Your best guide to when a bath is necessary should

CARE AND EQUIPMENT

be by using your eyes and nose!

Equipment

Your dog will require a collar and lead. The collar should be suitable for your type of dog and its age. Puppies should only wear soft fabric or leather collars. Your pet shop or dog trainer will be able to advise you what type of collar is suitable for your particular dog. The best type of lead without a doubt is a soft leather lead. These are far more expensive than fabric leads, but they last for years and are much kinder to your hands. Do not use leads consisting of a leather loop on a long chain as these are very uncomfortable to use and the chain can catch the dog in the face. No dog can pull hard enough to break a good leather lead.

Bowls for food and water are essential. Choose either lightweight metal bowls, as these are unbreakable and easy to keep clean, or earthenware bowls. Do not use plastic, as this is easily chewed or scratched and bacteria can develop on the scratched surface.

A bed is useful, although not essential. For a young puppy an old cardboard box with one side cut away and lined with a blanket is usually the cheapest option. All puppies chew, and you may well find that if you spend a lot of money on a posh bed it will soon be chewed to pieces. Choose a sturdy plastic bed, putting a blanket inside, or wait until the puppy has grown up before buying him a wicker basket or fabric bed. Dogs do need a soft area to sleep on, especially the large breeds, as they may otherwise develop calluses on their elbows. Do not let your dog sleep on a bare concrete floor.

Every dog, especially a pup, will appreciate some toys. Make sure that these do not come apart when they are chewed because the dog might swallow the pieces. Sterilised calcium bones are excellent for chewing too. If you let your dog play with a ball, make sure that it is large enough not to be swallowed. Accidents do happen when large dogs get small balls stuck in their throats. Never allow your dog to play with a stick or throw one for him. He might catch the stick awkwardly; this can damage his mouth or throat, or even kill him.

Grooming equipment is something that you will have to buy depending upon the breed. See the grooming section above, or ask your pet shop or groomer for advice. A pair of nail clippers designed for dogs is also a good investment.

Finally, no responsible owner should ever be without some sort of poop scoop. Various poop scoops are available from pet shops but personally I find that the cheapest and easiest method is to buy a packet of nappy sacks from the chemist. These are bags with large handles that are easy to tie together, and they are very cheap. Keep a supply in your pocket at all times. When your dog messes, simply pull a bag over your hand, pick up the mess, pull the bag over it, tie the handles together and dispose of the bag. These bags are even scented, which makes them ideal for the job!

BASIC TRAINING

Chapter 7 Basic training

All dogs need some basic training, whether they are tiny Yorkshire Terriers or large German Shepherds. A small dog may not be able to do much damage if he is badly trained and snaps at someone, nor will he be able to pull you over if he pulls hard on the lead, but it can be just as annoying. With children around, training is even more important. Your dog has to know that he must do as he is told by every member of the family, even the children. Also, training is great fun for both the dog and the family. My own children, at about the age of two started to copy me, telling the dogs to 'sit', 'stay' and 'come'. This chapter is only a brief introduction to the very basics in dog training. For more information, read a specialist book on the subject, or contact your local dog training club (details of registered clubs can be obtained from The Kennel Club).

House training

The very first lesson that any puppy needs to be taught is to be clean inside the house. House training should start the moment you arrive home with your new puppy. It is difficult to say how long it will take to get your puppy house trained; some are clean in a couple of weeks whilst others take longer. An eight-week-old puppy is unable to refrain from

41

BASIC TRAINING

BASIC TRAINING

urinating for more than an hour or so at a time and you should not have great expectations from a young puppy. Most puppies will be reliably house trained by the age of 4–5 months with, perhaps, the odd accident during the night. Compare it to potty training a child: it does not happen overnight.

The key to getting your puppy clean is to be vigilant. Every time he has had a game, been asleep or has eaten, pick him up and carry him outside. Wait with him, do not leave him on his own. Use a command such as 'Busy' or 'Be clean' and, once he has done his business, praise him in a really happy voice so that he understands that he has done something clever. If he has an accident indoors, simply ignore it. He must never be punished for relieving himself indoors because he will not understand what he has done wrong. Indeed, he may associate the punishment with the acts of urinating and defecating and start to 'go' in hidden places where he will not be discovered, such as behind a chair or under a table.

The puppy may be used to going on newspaper at the breeder's, so leave newspapers out for him, ideally placed by the back door and not too close to his bed. No dog likes to mess near where he sleeps. When the puppy needs to relieve himself, you will notice that he starts to walk around in tight circles. You can then pick him up quickly and place him on the papers, if you are not quick enough to get him outside. Usually it only takes a day or two before the puppy realises what the papers are for and, as the papers are close to the back door, you will soon notice when the puppy goes to the door and you can let him out. Be vigilant and the whole process will be a quick one.

Recognising his name

The next lesson is for the puppy to learn to recognise his name and to come when he is called. Use his name whenever you play with him and talk to him, and encourage the children to do the same. Children are a great help here. The trick is to get the puppy to associate his name with pleasant events, such as being cuddled or played with, or with food. It should not need to take more than a day to teach the puppy his name.

To get the puppy to come when he is called (the most important lesson any dog must learn), remember never to let him associate his name with a bad experience. If you are telling the puppy off for some reason, do not use his name. Say 'bad dog' instead.

If you are out in the park with the puppy off his lead, do not just call him to put the lead back on. If you do, he will learn to associate being called with having his freedom restricted. Young puppies are eager to follow their owners, and worry about losing sight of them. Use this to your advantage. Run away from your puppy, calling his name. Hide behind a tree or bush, calling him. The puppy will soon learn that he needs to keep his eyes on you or you may disappear. This is how it should be; the dog keeping his eyes on you to make sure you are there, not you constantly having to watch out to see if the dog has run off.

During each walk, call the dog several times. Every time the dog comes to you, praise him, cuddle him, play with him, and really exaggerate your happiness at seeing him. Then let him go again. If you start this process early enough, the dog will learn to associate you with fun, and he will think that being with you is far more fun than running off without you. I have lost count of the number of people I have met during my dog walks who simply cannot get their dogs to come when they are called. Such dogs are a liability as they may

BASIC TRAINING

BASIC TRAINING

run up to people who are frightened of dogs, run into a road and cause an accident, or approach an aggressive dog that then attacks them. It is all caused by incorrect training.

Many people advise dog owners to reward the dog with treats when he responds to being called. Personally I find that this is counter-productive as then the dog will come only if he feels that food is more interesting than anything else he can see, such as another dog. Dogs are not always hungry.

The dog should learn to come when called because he loves his owner. Never punish your dog for having run off. If he doesn't come when called, and you wait and wait for him to finally come, then it is very easy to tell him off when he does return. But look at it from his point of view: he came to you and was punished! Where's the incentive in coming back to you the next time you call? If your dog fails to respond, always run in the opposite direction to him. Jump about, make funny noises, anything to get his attention. If trained properly, your dog will always respond to being called, and can then be allowed a lot of freedom off the lead.

Wearing a collar and lead

This is another early lesson that every puppy needs to be taught. Most puppies will object to this to start with. Make sure that you have a plain, light collar that won't bother your puppy too much and put this on first. Play with him to distract him and he will soon get used to the idea. He will probably kick at the collar with his hindlegs to start with in an attempt to get it off, but this will soon stop. Then you are ready to clip the lead on and, again, use a light puppy lead for the first few sessions.

It is perfectly possible to start practising this indoors or in your back garden. Take hold of the lead but do not pull on it. If you do, your puppy will sit and refuse to move or he may even start to jump about. Simply follow him around on a loose lead to start with. After a little while, start to coax the puppy into following you by calling his name whilst you walk backwards. He will soon start to follow you and in no time at all you will have a dog that walks on the lead.

This is the time to make sure that your dog never starts pulling on his lead because this can be a real nuisance, especially if he is a large breed. Again, if taught correctly when young, your dog need never develop any bad habits. Should he pull forward on the lead, so that the lead becomes tight, give a slight jerk on it and pull him back with a command such as 'steady'. As long as you never allow him to pull ahead, he will never get into the habit of doing it. All dogs should be able to walk on a slack lead on the left side of their owner. I have seven dogs that I can walk on my own without being pulled over, so you see that it is quite possible to have a dog that does not pull.

Socialisation

Socialisation is another very important part of a puppy's upbringing. This means getting the puppy used to everyday life, both inside and outside the house. As soon as your puppy has completed his course of vaccinations, start taking him out and about. Do not worry if he is too young or small to walk; carry him instead. Bring him to many places, such as into town, on the bus, close to roads and so on, so that he gets the opportunity to encounter lots of new situations. Talk to him calmly at all times and praise him for behaving. Allow him to meet other people and other friendly dogs.

BASIC TRAINING

If you wait until he is older before doing all this, you will find that he will be terrified of unknown situations and, whereas it is easy to cope with a 12-week-old puppy that panics at the sight of a car, it will be much more difficult to calm him down when he is six months old and nearly full size. Puppies that are allowed to encounter lots of new situations will grow up to be friendly and confident dogs.

Basic commands

Some basic commands that your dog needs to be taught should include 'sit', 'leave', 'down', and 'stay'. This is the very minimum that any dog should be taught, together with the all-important 'come', of course.

Nowadays it is very popular to train dogs by using treats, rewarding them for doing something right. However, not all dogs respond to this as some simply are not that interested in food, and others may be so excited by the smell of food that they cannot concentrate. I do not use food rewards when training any dog; just plenty of vocal praise, stroking and cuddling the dog when he does right. This works perfectly well and makes for a happy and well-behaved dog that is behaving for one reason only – the love of his owner.

BASIC TRAINING

Sit
To teach 'sit', simply push the puppy's bottom firmly to the ground, at the same time as saying 'sit'. As soon as the puppy sits, praise him and allow him to get up. If this is done correctly, you can teach a puppy to sit in a day.

Down
The 'down' command is very similar to 'sit', and is a useful exercise as, for example, it means that you can tell your dog to go and lie down. With the dog in the sitting position, firmly press on his shoulders and say 'down'. Most puppies will slide down immediately. If the puppy resists, pull his front legs out in front of him gently. As soon as he is down, praise him. Again, this exercise needn't take long to teach. Remember never to tell your dog to 'sit down', as then he will be very confused, as 'sit' and 'down' will mean two different things to him.

Stay
'Stay' can mean the difference between life and death, as it can be used to stop the dog from running across a road. You can also teach your dog to stay while you pick up his mess during a walk, with both hands free to do so. To teach the 'stay', start with the dog on a lead, in either the sit or down position. Say 'stay' firmly, and hold the palm of your hand in front of the dog's face. Then take one step away from him, and one step only. If the dog stays put, move back to him and praise him. If he moves towards you, place him in the original position and start again. You can then start to move further away but be sure to make it a gradual process. Eventually your dog will be able to do the exercise off the lead.

Leave
Teaching your dog what 'leave' means is also very important as you will be able to tell him, for example, not to touch the children's toys. With the dog on a lead, place a tempting object on the ground. Walk past it and, as the dog turns towards it, say 'leave' and pull him away. Repeat this until he understands the meaning of the word.

Dog training classes
Most towns have dog training clubs or classes and it is an excellent idea to join such a class. By doing so, you will get expert help in training your dog, and this will have the added advantage of your dog learning to behave even when in the company of other dogs and people. Why not take the whole family along, too? It is usually best if only one person has the main responsibility for the dog's training, but the rest of the family can come along to watch and learn. Training classes are for everyone and children as young as eight are usually allowed to take part alongside older children and adults. Dog training classes are often advertised in local papers (your vet may know of some), and often The Kennel Club can put you in touch with local clubs.

Index

A
adult dogs 5, 21, 23

B
babies 32
bed 27, 32, 34, 40
bedrooms 28
breeders . . . . 19 - 20

C
collar 27, 45
company 4, 7
costs 8
crate 27
crossbreeds 21

D
'down' 47

E
equipment 40
exercise . . . . 5, 6, 33, 37 - 38

F
fleas 36
food 34, 36
food bowls 27, 40

G
grooming . . . . 38 - 40
gundog group 11, 12

H
health 24, 26, 36
hereditary diseases 10
hound group 11
house training . . . . 4, 41 - 43

K
Kennel Club, The 20

L
lead 40, 45
lead training 45
'leave' 47

M
meal times 36
mongrels 10, 21

N
name 43
neutering . . . . 23 - 24

P
pastoral group 16
pedigree dogs . . . . 10 - 11
pet insurance 36
poop scoop 32, 40
puppy farms 19

R
rescue dogs 5, 21, 23
rescue organisations 21
Royal Society for the Prevention
  of Cruelty to Animals (RSPCA) 21

S
selection . . . . 19 - 26
'sit' 47
socialisation 23, 45
'stay' 47

T
temperament . . . . 10 - 11, 19, 26
terrier group 13
titbits 37, 46
toddlers 35
toxocariasis 32
toy group 14
toys 27, 40
training . . . . 41 - 47
training classes 47

U
utility group 14

V
vaccinations 36
veterinary surgeon 31, 36

W
working group . . . . 17 - 18
worming 20, 36